The Wall

Images and Offerings
from the
Vietnam Veterans Memorial

Conceived by Sal Lopes
Introduction by Michael Norman

A Floyd Yearout Production

Collins Publishers

Lines reprinted on page 13 are from "Little Gidding, Four Quartets"
© T. S. Eliot. They are reprinted by permission of Harcourt Brace
Jovanovich Inc.

Lines reprinted on page 44 are from "The Wall That Brought Us Together"
© 1984 Robert E. Fleetwood. They are reprinted by permission of
the author.

Lines reprinted on page 72 are from "The Name Is On A Monument, The Words
Are In A Heart" © 1982 Igor Bobrowsky. They are reprinted by permission of
the author.

"The Invasion of Grenada" on page 121 © 1984 W. D. Ehrhart from *To Those Who
Have Gone Home Tired: New & Selected Poems*, published by Thunder's Mouth
Press. It is reprinted by permission of the author.

First published 1987 by Collins Publishers, Inc., New York.

Library of Congress Cataloging-in-Publication Data
Main entry under title: The Wall: Images and Offerings from the Vietnam
Veterans Memorial.

Lopes, Sal.
The wall: images and offerings from the Vietnam Veterans Memorial.

"A Floyd Yearout Production."
1. Vietnam Veterans Memorial (Washington, D.C.)—Pictorial works.
2. Washington (D.C.)—Buildings, structures, etc.—Pictorial works.
3. Washington (D.C.)—Description—1981—Views.
I. Title

F203.4.V54L67 1987 959.704'36 87-10375
ISBN 0-00-217974-1

Art Director: Thomas K. Walker

Printed in Japan   First Printing: August 1987

10 9 8 7 6 5 4 3 2 1

Editors' Note

The existence of *The Wall* is testimony to the extraordinary power the Vietnam Veterans Memorial has on those who visit it. Five years ago, on the day the memorial was dedicated, freelance photographer Sal Lopes made his first pilgrimage to the nation's newest shrine. "I owed it to four close friends of mine who sacrificed their lives," says Lopes. Since that day, in November 1982, Lopes has journeyed from his Massachusetts home more than two dozen times to photograph the Wall and the people who commune there with the dead and the living.

Sal Lopes' passion for the Wall and the intense human emotion captured in his photographs reveal to us the magic of this memorial, which in five short years has become a kind of national wailing wall.

The Wall: Images and Offerings from the Vietnam Veterans Memorial, photographed by Lopes and 16 other photojournalists, documents the powerful spell that the memorial holds on its visitors. Amongst these photographic images are excerpts of letters, notes and fragments of communication left at the Wall by families, friends and comrades of the 58,132 dead and missing whose names are engraved there.

It is important to note that no specific relationship exists between individual photographs and writings. We tried to create for the reader feelings similar to those experienced by a visitor to the Wall—a sense of timelessness and reflectiveness, often mixed with spontaneous outpourings of emotion. All of the letters and quotes included in *The Wall* were left at the Vietnam Veterans Memorial. We have obtained the approval of those who wrote them or, failing to locate an author, have excerpted only small portions and maintained the writer's anonymity.

As our own offering to the Wall, at the time of publication, and with each subsequent reprinting of this book, we are making a donation to the Friends of the Vietnam Veterans Memorial, a nonprofit organization that provides information about the monument and promotes understanding of the historical and emotional legacy of the Vietnam conflict.

Brennon Jones and Amy Janello
Collins Publishers

...ALBROU...

...GRANE... DANNIE J BREWIN...

JAMES R CROLEY... JE...

...DILLARD... JACK M BROWN Jr...

...ROBERT W RUHL • DALLAS E G...

...ND J JACKSON... ALLEN L JELINEK...

...LONG • LEROY BARNES... MICHA...

...NEWMAN • LEROY E PETERSON •...

...Jr • JOSE C GOSSE • BERNARD A...

...YL G WINTERS • STEPHEN A ZUKO...

...CAMPBELL • S W GEORGE • TIMO...

...ILKINS • CLIFFORD L CARPENTER...

...ES • ROLF W JORGENSEN • BILLY...

...EWIS... ERNEST D MITCHEL...

...EST • MICHAEL R SMITH •
GH • HEARNE W BEAVER • JAMES BESC
GTON ★ JOHN T DOIKE • THOMAS J BU
SUS DE LA ROSA Jr • TERRY A DENNISON
CHARLES R FLEMING ★ CHARLES L GET
EEN ★ BOBBY ROY HOLLEY • DAVID W
RAYMOND E JOHNSON • THOMAS B
L J MUMMEL ★ CHARLES A McGUIRK •
ATRICK T QUINN • JAMES M RADZELO
GREEN • TURNER L THOMPSON Jr •
V • JAMES F ASKIN • CLIFFORD S BRAT
HY S DAVIES • DAVID A DILLON •
BRENT I GRIGGS • EDWARD F HAR
NELSON • DOUGI

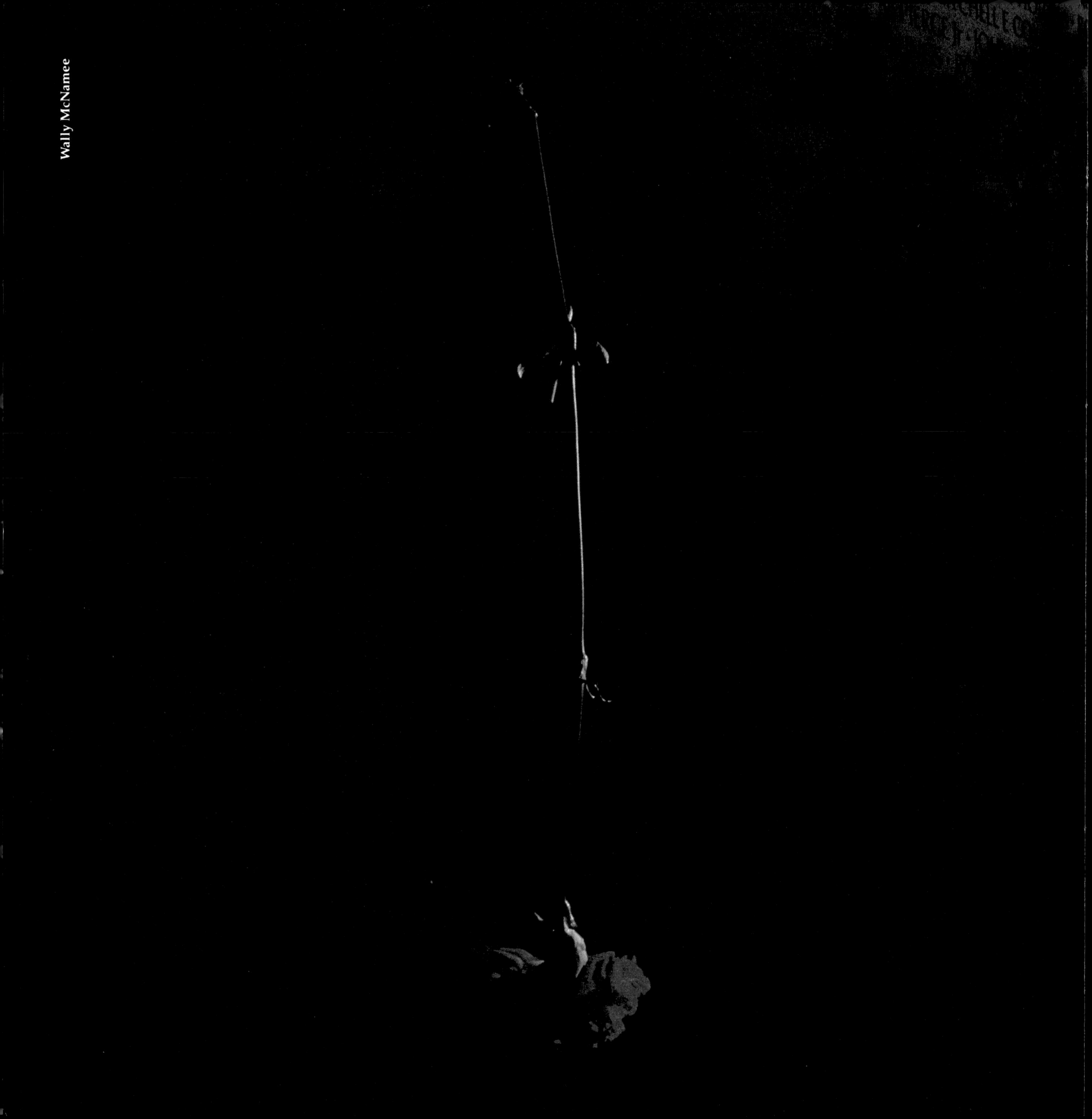

Wally McNamee

Damn you brother - why didn't you
come back? I want you back, but not
in a box. I still love you and I'd love
you if you came back in one piece or
your arms or legs or mind gone. I wasn't
that young when you died because I
cried too. God has you now but I want
you too so damn you for not coming back.

Sal Lopes

We die with the dying:
See, they depart, and we go with them.
We are born with the dead:
See, they return, and bring us with them.

T. S. Eliot
Little Gidding, Four Quartets

Introduction

They walk as if on hallowed ground. They touch the stone. They speak with the dead. They come to mourn and to remember, memory mixing with grief, making an old ritual new, creating in this time another timeless moment.

Seeing this, coming upon it at dawn or in the melancholy drizzle of a winter solstice, it is hard to remember that no one is buried there, that the long chevron of black granite is a memorial, not a sprawling cairn on a common grave.

It is a sad place—there is no denying that—especially sad for the volunteers and luckless conscripts who survived the war, men like me, trying to make sense of the senseless, trying to find a way to remember that will not mock the meaning of the dead.

Some men who cross the years and struggle home say they need no memorial to keep alive the memory of those cut down beside them. This is true, and yet I am pleased to see it there, stretched out under the sky a stone's throw from the Potomac River, there where Lincoln talks of the dead to "us the living."

The memorial is a way back and a way forward. A pass through Constitution Gardens and a walk along "The Wall" makes us think of the future in the language of the past and whatever message one draws from this, it seems unlikely that anyone who makes that walk will be able to think of war and the men who fight it in quite the same way again.

In honor of the men and women of the Armed Forces of the United States who served in the Vietnam War. The names of those who gave their lives and of those who remain missing are inscribed in the order they were taken from us.

Fifty-eight thousand, one hundred and thirty-two names photo-stenciled—etched—chronologically in the order of their deaths onto two walls, each 246.75 feet long, that meet at an angle of 125 degrees. The walls begin roughly at ground level and, at the vertex, rise to the height of 10.1 feet. Each wall has 70 panels cut from black granite mined in a quarry near Bangalore, India, and polished to form a surface that reflects the sky and the ground and those who stand before it. Nearby is a flagpole with an American flag and an eight-foot bronze statue of three infantrymen staring off roughly in the direction of the granite roll call.

The Wall was designed by the most unlikely of architects, Maya Ying Lin, a woman of Asian descent, who knew nothing of war. In 1981, when she submitted her design to a competition held by the Vietnam Veterans Memorial Fund, she was 21 years old, an architecture student at Yale University:

I had designed the memorial for a seminar on funerary architecture....We had already been questioning what a war memorial is, its purpose, its responsibility....I felt a memorial should be honest about the reality of war and be for the people who gave their lives....I didn't want a static object that people would just look at, but something they could relate to as on a journey, or passage, that would bring each to his own conclusions....I had an impulse to cut open the earth... an initial violence that in time would heal....It was as if the black-brown earth were polished and made into an interface between the sunny world and the quiet dark world beyond, that we can't enter....The names would become the memorial. There was no need to embellish.

Opinion over the design, just as it had been over the war, was divided, and during the memorial's planning stages in 1981, this political and aesthetic skirmishing threatened to kill the project. The memorial was conceived by Jan C. Scruggs, then a 31-year-old former infantryman who saw combat in Vietnam. He wanted a people's memorial financed entirely by contributions. In the end, he would raise some $7 million—money from unions and veterans' organizations and corporations, money from the men, women and children of the United States, 275,000 contributions in all.

Scruggs' memorial committee won congressional support for a bill setting aside two acres of land in Washington's Constitution Gardens in the shadow of the Lincoln Memorial. Then the committee selected a jury of architects and sculptors to hold a design competition. When entry number 1026 won, the skirmishing began.

Tom Carhart, a veteran who had entered the design competition, called Maya Lin's memorial "a black gash of shame," a phrase that became a rallying call for the opposition. Author Jim Webb, a Marine Corps combat veteran, thought the Wall did little to lift the spirits of the men who fought in Vietnam: "It was not supposed to be the Vietnam Dead Memorial. Art is a metaphor and the metaphorical statement of it is absolutely negative." In the end, with the bronze statue and flagpole added as a compromise, Maya Lin's design won official approval.

"It is a subtle design, like every great memorial capable of being given different meanings by each of us," wrote Paul Goldberger, the architecture critic of *The New York Times*. "The anguish of the Vietnam War is present here but not in a way that does any dishonor to veterans….This memorial…honors the veterans who served in Vietnam with more poignancy, surely, than any ordinary monument ever could."

It was the public, of course, who made the final judgment on the people's memorial. Between 4 and 5 million came by the site in 1986, making it, perhaps, the most visited outdoor memorial in the nation's capital.

Gold Star Mothers look for the names of their sons, young children, the names of their fathers. Friends and family come, a second cousin from Calumet, a classmate from Iowa City. Generations pass by the Wall, one too young to have known the war, another too old to have fought it. Men and women in uniform come, some salute, some just stare. Tourists come by the busload, snapping pictures as they file by. Solitary figures come, standing silently off to one side, drifting back in memory.

And then there are the veterans.

Some 9 million men and women were in uniform between 1965 and 1975; 1.3 million are believed to have seen combat. Nearly 300,000 men were wounded in the war, 75,000 of them disabled by their wounds. There is no final count on the number of other casualties, the ones who returned with scars on their psyches or deadly toxins in their blood.

The veterans arrive at their memorial walking and in wheelchairs, in three-piece suits and old jungle fatigues. They wear their hats, they wear their boots, they wear their medals. Almost always they weep. Oh, how we weep, "…cursing and sobbing and thinking of the dead," wrote Robert Graves.

We mourn the many, we mourn the one, perhaps the first man we saw fall, perhaps the friend who took our place on patrol. I have such a name, panel 50 east, line 52, Andrew James Payne, Jr., a member of

Charlie Squad, 1st Platoon, Golf Company, 2nd Battalion, 9th Marines, killed April 19, 1968.

Jim had grown up in the sun—red hair, freckles, a mouth full of gleaming white teeth. He played base-ball and football and chess. He had a paper route and sold road flares and styrofoam snowmen at Christmas. He studied at Hoover High, drove a vintage 1950 black Ford jalopy, and lived at home on Thompson Street in Glendale, California, with three brothers and a sister.

He was killed on the morning of a hot day on a dusty road near Khe Sanh, shot in the stomach by an enemy he could not see. He sat in the sun against a rock, bleeding to death while his comrades tried to finish the fight. He may have died for his country or for his God or for nothing at all. For a long time, I thought he died for me.

It is hard to remember that no one is buried there. The memorial is a collection point, an altar upon which the living leave tokens of the dead and trappings for an afterlife:

Here is a can of beer or a tin of sardines—"remember how he loved them so." And here is a single blood-red rose, cradled in baby's breath, white and soft. Purple Hearts and discharge papers and uniforms are here—military trappings for a military death. A model ship, a stuffed bear, a key chain, and a toy soldier. T-shirts, travel kits, flight jackets and flags.

They leave letters too, messages sent across the void:

"I took the solemn walk past this monument of black granite for you this day…."

"I just wanted to come here today to tell you I love you…."

"I'm so sorry Frankie—I know we left you—I hope you didn't suffer too much—give them hell—…."

So many letters and so many artifacts have been left—more than 4,900 at last count—that the act of leaving something behind has become a ritual at the memorial. Officials of the National Park Service, which maintains the memorial and collects and catalogs the artifacts at a climate-controlled warehouse in Lanham, Maryland, say the collection is now a memorial in itself, a remembrance of sacrifice apart from the lodestone of black polished granite on a quiet capital green.

Veterans Day 1987 is the fifth anniversary of the Vietnam Veterans Memorial. The controversy over the design has quieted now. Six months after the dedication, in May 1983, President Reagan made his first visit to the memorial and in so doing the commander-in-chief gave it the official sanction the fighting men of Vietnam had so long sought.

Looking back across the five years and all that has been said and written about that spectral place, the first description of the memorial, the words of the designer, seems most apt. Maya Lin said she wanted to create a journey, a passage, and indeed she has.

To follow the Wall from ground level to its vertex is to walk down into the past. As the long polished panels reflect those who move before them, the names of the past become etched on the faces of the present and, for a moment, the living and the dead are one.

To go to the Wall is thus to be a part of history, "to mingle," as Stephen Crane wrote, "in one of those great affairs of the earth." Perhaps this is part of the memorial's appeal: for the uninitiated, it is a way to get a sense of the experience they have only read about or have seen flickering on a small screen. But it is also more than this because the Wall has brought war home in a way television never could. Here is the mystery of death writ in stone 58,132 times. For the living, the mystery was never more palpable.

To touch the Wall is to touch the dead, to get close to them. And as they make this crossing—as those who never knew war come close to those taken by it—they begin to understand Vietnam and thus honor the generation of veterans who survived the war.

We have never asked for more than that.

Michael Norman
Montclair, N.J.
February 1987

Jodi Cobb

Nick Sebastian

If I could, I would lead each person in hand past this monument and make them read each name and imagine each life that was cut short.

Dear Bill,

Today, I come to this memorial, this black wall. I come to put flowers and a letter, not because it's a special day, like your birthday or Memorial Day. But just because it's Tuesday, and just because I love and miss you so and want the whole world to know.

The other day I saw a picture of Elvis Presley on a poster in a music store window. Under his picture it read, "Remember I lived, forget I died." I stood looking at this for a long time, wondering how you could possibly forget that someone you loved so much had died.

Yes, I remember that you lived. I remember our laughter together and our tears when your rabbits died and especially when your grandparents died. I remember when you would get mad at me because you had to do the dishes or carry out the trash or be in bed a certain time on school nights.

But I can't forget that you died. I will never forget the day I heard of your death. I will never forget the long days of waiting for your body to be returned from Vietnam. I will never forget the millions of tears I have shed. And I can't forget the terrible hurt because you are not with me and never will be again.

I have cried many, many tears since you left us because I saw no reason for you to die then and I see no reason now.

But this I do know, you are happier with God in heaven than you could ever be on earth. So forgive me, my son, my Billy, when I cry because most of my tears are for me, I guess, because you are not with me and I miss you so.

Mom

Bob,

I bring you a message from Sandy. She still loves you! She still remembers you! You'll always be her love!

Here's a slide and photo of Tom. In case you find his name,
I thought it would be nice for you to know him a little.

He was one of those special friends that one gets to know
only occasionally in a lifetime. Nineteen years old, with everything to live for. Loved the Four Seasons music and was born
and raised in Battle Creek, Michigan.

Being his best friend, I tried desperately to get to him before he died, but was unable to. I've always felt really bad about
this, so if you find him, tell him I'm really sorry I couldn't get to
him in time. And I promise I will get to the memorial in person
sometime in the future.

If you can't find his name, please don't worry about it. It
really is something I have to do personally when I can. Thanks
a lot for looking, though.

Sal Lopes

You were the only young man from our town to die in the
Vietnam War, and not the best boy the town produced—more
like a hoodlum most of the time.

But you did not shirk your duty nor did you take the "easy"
route to Canada. As a result you made the ultimate sacrifice.
You might not have cared about your little home town, but in
your way, you helped to keep it free.

There is no monument to record your sacrifice, nor is your
name read out on Memorial Day. Some of us think of you once
in a while, though. Whenever I'm home from the army, I visit
your gravesite.

From all of us, thanks.

I came down today to pay respects to two good friends of mine. Go down and visit them sometime. They are on panel 42E, lines 22 and 26. I think you will like them.

35

Finally, America has awakened and taken home those of us who live and remember you and all the others....I kept your spirit alive till America woke up, Sir. I'm done. Rest well my friend, my Lieutenant.

38

1959

Your name is on a black wall in D.C., but I'm sorry to say that it's a little below ground, kind of like how Charlie was!

You overlook a nice green, a place like where we used to play football back home.

A lot of people walk by all day. You can tell which are the vets. We are the ones who don't have to ask about the size or type of material used to make the wall. We just stand and look, not caring who sees us cry, just like no one cared who died.

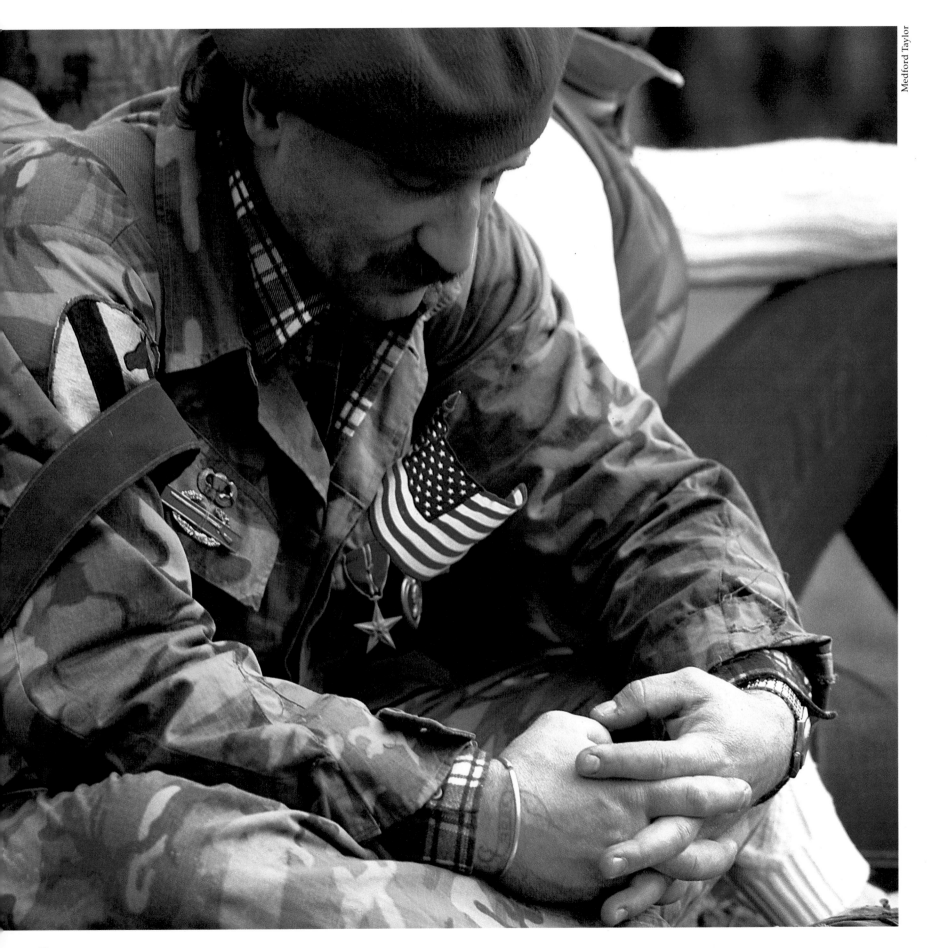

43

May that silent wall shout out for peace as we all should now
and forever. For while most walls keep people apart, it's the
wall that brought us together.

Sal Lopes

I never cried. My chest becomes unbearably painful and my
throat tightens so I can't even croak, but I haven't cried.
I wanted to, just couldn't. I think I can today. Damn, I'm crying
now. Bye Smitty. Get some rest.

You and I were not friends while you were alive, but then we were only kids. I came today to honor your sacrifice. I came for Kathy and your parents, but also for the man you would have grown to be. A man I would have liked.

The kid I remember probably wouldn't have cared much for these flowers from my garden, but the man you could have been would appreciate them. The Indian blanket and purple sage are native to Texas and there are sprigs of thyme, melissa and fennel native to your father's homeland.

Sal Lopes

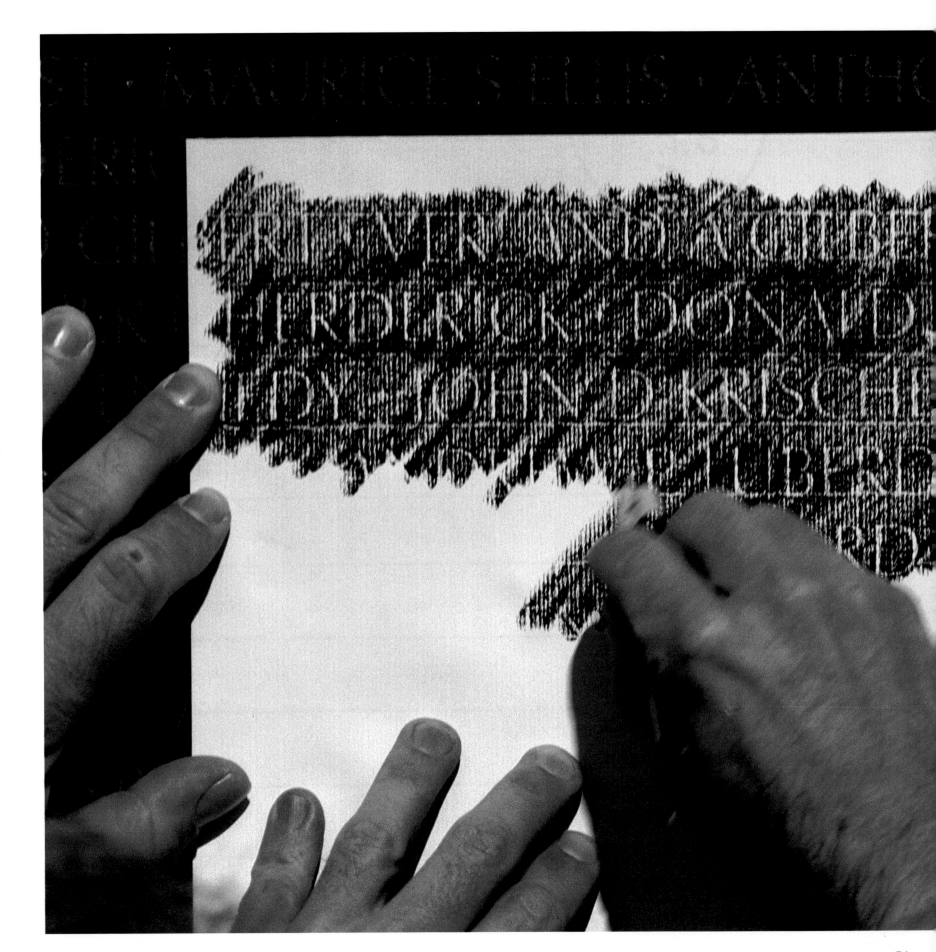

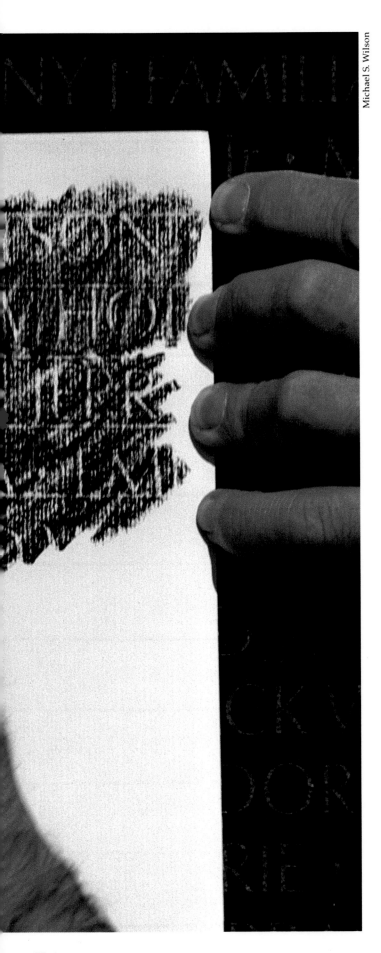

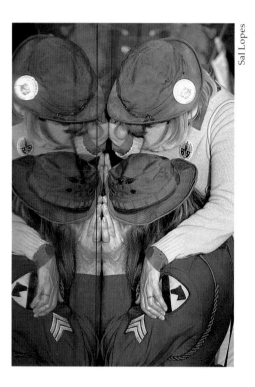

Sal Lopes

We did what we could but it was not enough because I found you here. You are not just a name on this wall. You are alive. You are blood on my hands. You are screams in my ears. You are eyes in my soul.

I told you you'd be all right, but I lied, and please forgive me. I see your face in my son, I can't bear the thought. You told me about your wife, your kids, your girl, your mother. And then you died. Your pain is mine. I'll never forget your face. I can't.

You are still alive.

THOMAS A MANCINO · GARY W MARTINI · JIMMY M MULLINS
JAMES L OWENS · BRUCE C PARMELEE
LARRY C PETTAWAY · GARY D GRIMES
JAMES H SHELTON
GEORGE F VOLK · JOHN W WALL
JOSEPH D WYLIE III · JIMMIE D CINTRON
DAVID W WINTERS
LOUIS F CERRANO Jr · JAMES R ADAMS
ARNOLD L BROCK
JAMES P ENGLISH · OTTO R ENSSLIN
JAMES B EASTERLING
ALLEN L GARDNER · ANDREW L HAMILTON · MARSHALL H ISBELL
PHILLIP A MOORE · DOUGLAS H McCALL
RAUL BAUTISTA PEREZ · WESLEY J PIZER · WILLIAM A PROCTOR
PAUL L STIMPSON · RAYMOND R TURNER
HENRY L WEAVER · EUGENE E WEST · ADAM D BALLARD
HOWARD BULLARD · STEPHEN L COLOPY · JOSEPH F DALY
JIMMIE HOWARD · DAVID ALVES · LAWRENCE F LEWELLIN
JAMES L RUSSELL · FREDERICK C SCHMIDT · ROBERT C STEPHENSON
GARY W WELCH · EDWARD W WELLS · DOUGLAS B HAMILTON
RAUL CASAREZ · RAYMOND S CASSIDY · JUSTINO E CASTRO-RAMOS
ARMANDO GALLARDO · RICHARD L HADNOT · RONALD L BARBER
KENT A LEONARD · CLIVE V MOSIER · BRADLEY A NELSON
TORRES PEREZ · JAMES C POMERLEAU · GEORGE T POWELL · PHILIP H SAUER
STEWART · JACK L SUTTON · EDWIN B TUCKER · RAYMOND L TWOMEY
LARRY GENE BONNELL · JERRY CAPE · DALE E CARMICHAEL
ROBERT L WESKAMP · GARY L DOOSE · TERRANCE D FRYE
MICHAEL G GIBBS · MELVIN L GREEN · JAMES W HAMILTON Jr
LATIMER · JAMES V LAWLOR · JOSEPH M LINGLE Jr · RONALD L LYVERE
CHARLES M NEAL Jr · STEPHEN C NELSON · RICHARD C PRATT
EDWARD G SHARPE · LEONARD H SMITH · ROBERT J STERLING
JOHN G CURTIN · JOSHUA A ATKINS III · CHARLES D AUSTIN
FRED E BARNETTE · THOMAS M BARROW Jr · DONALD L BERNARD
RICHARD T BROWN · LARRY W BUTLER · DANA C DARNELL
SHELLY EGLY · MICHAEL J ESTOCIN · EMMANUEL S FENECH
FRANCISCO · LARRY F GEIGER · GUY C GETTINGS · LINDY R HALL
TILLMON P HITCHCOCK · ISAAC JONES · LEONARD O LA PORT
MALONEY · WILLIAM M MEYER · WALTER F MORRIS · JAMES F MURRAY
KENNETH W ORTON Jr · DAVID R PAGE · HERMAN H PAYNE
THOMAS A PREAUX · KERMIT A RAY
DANIEL L KIRSTEIN
JOHN E LANING · JAMES L LESTER
ROBERT L MARGOLIS
CLYDE E NEWMAN
JOSE ANTONIO ROSAS
ROBERT D SELLS Jr
KURT C STAAB
MELVIN A WADE
JOHN E YOUNG
LAYNE F CLIFTON
WILLIAM E CZARNY
RICHARD A HEIN
RONNIE RAY LANDERS
JAMES M QUIGLEY
RONALD M STEIN · LYLE S TATE
RAUL VILLA · CHARLES R WALLER
HEINZ AHLMEYER Jr
HUGH F BLACKBURN
LUTHER CHAMBLISS
RICHARD J DAVIS
JOHN D GILGENBERG
BRIAN C HEWITT
JOHN T KLOC · ELDON F KRIEGER
PAUL T LOONEY
LEONARD E NISKI
JAMES C RILEY · MARCELINO
ROBERT L SNYDER
DONALD A PITTENGER
STERLING S WOODS
FRANCIS J DUFFY
JOSEPH T MARTIN
RICHARD L BASINGER
WILLIAM F CLOVER Jr
PAUL R EDINGTON
JOHN M GEARY

Jodi Cobb

This marks the second year I have come to the Wall. I have seen the names of those I know, and, yes, I have cried. My problem is I don't know the names of those I tried to help only to have them die in my arms....

In Vietnam, at age 20, I was put in charge of a riverboat. Now everytime I get on a boat, I only see the red blood running over the deck and into the water. I try to take my two sons fishing, but we never stay out long. The fish don't seem to bite when I take them out like they do when they go with someone else's father. They are too young to understand that their father does not like the reflections he sees in the water.

For these reasons I write to say I'm sorry....I did the best I could. To all you mothers, fathers, brothers, sisters, wives and lovers of those men, I am sorry. *"I could do no more...."*

I wish I knew your names so I could touch your names in the black stone. But I don't and I'm sorry. *"So sorry."*

Attached to this letter are my service medals. These belong to you and your family and friends. I don't need them to show I was there. I have your faces to remind me in my sleep....

Rest well my brothers, may the wind be to your backs and the sun in your faces. On the day we meet again please do one thing. "Tell me your name."

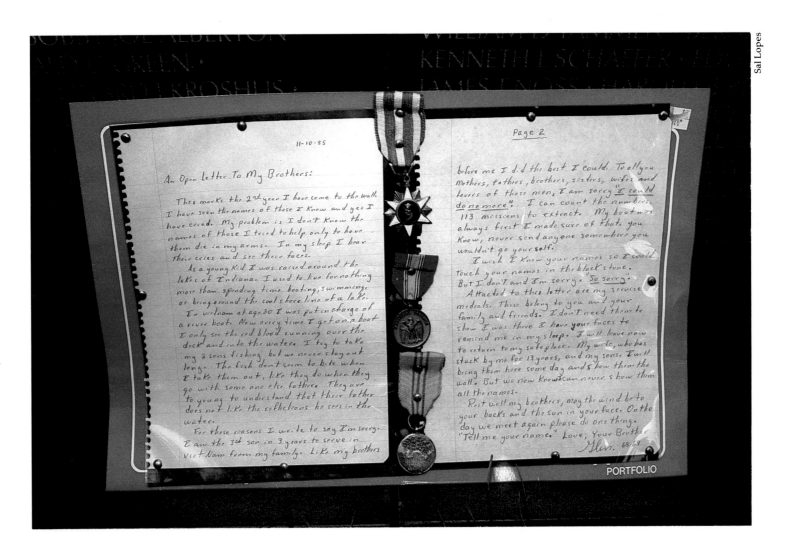

PORTFOLIO

I'm bringing Teddy bear and a picture of your loved race car.
I realize they can't stay there long but they are yours and I want
them to be with you.

Dad,

It's nearly impossible to write what I feel today. I may never know why things happened the way they did. I wish to hell I did.

Someday you may come home and I'll know then the truth. I wish you could reach me and tell me what happened.

You have grandchildren now. They know of you and they love you.

Someday we'll be together again and maybe then we can do all those things we never could before.

I love and miss you,
Gary

Still don't know why.
Think you guys may be better off.
Strange?

I shut my eyes and wouldn't listen when they came with morning and told me that you had slipped away. I closed my mind against my thoughts, not wanting to believe you'd gone. Not dragged off, captured in the bright day's savage madness, not overwhelmed by the dark blind angers of the night, but here, within the sight and sound and smell and feel of sea, of salty spray on gentle winds so near.

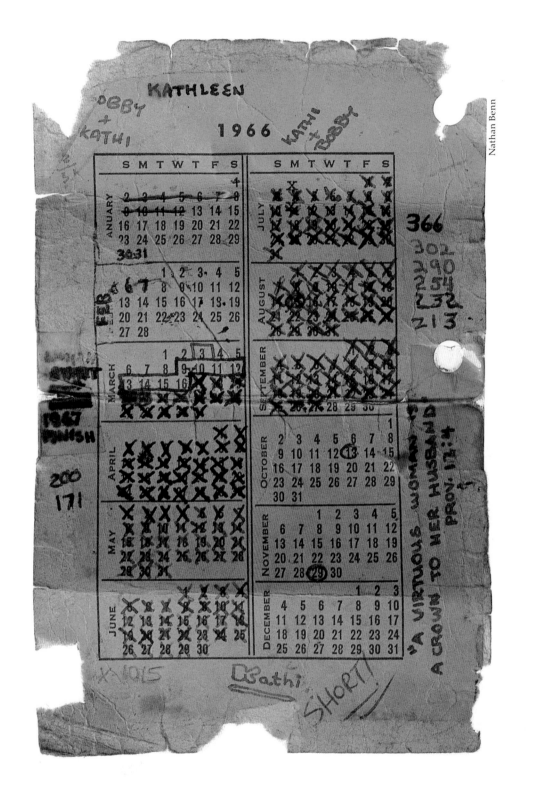

Dear Gary, Doug and Billy,

Well, that time has rolled around and the class of '65 is having its 20-year reunion. Cheers, cheers for old Orchard Park High School.

Don't be afraid that you will not be remembered. We all talked about you in 1975 and our thoughts are still with you.

Doug, they moved your house off the boulevard onto a new street. Your death was a real shock—especially since you were so adamant about hating guns.

Billy, I'm sorry we never lived out the fantasy of running into each other in a supermarket with batches of children.

And, yes, Gary, I still talk too much.

I had to come here. I live in Los Angeles now and I could not have gone to that reunion without first coming.

Eli Reed

Sal Lopes

Now I am grown and I look a lot like you. Who would
have known I would grow up to look like someone I never
even knew.

1st DIV. 2/28th INF "B" CO "VIETNAM 1965"

LONNIE A. PANGBURN
103 N. KENNEDY ROAD

Sal Lopes

In 1968 we spent some time together. We tried not to get close, but for reasons only you and I can understand, we did.

We laughed, drank beer, played cards and even cried together. Our camp was open to you and yours to us.

I remember how safe I felt knowing we had you close by to help us get through those horrible nights. There were so many nights I watched the tracer rounds and mortars enter your camp. How helpless I felt wondering and praying if we could make it just one day closer to our time to come home.

Terror was in the air. To this day I recall the smell and taste of it. The memories are the worst, from seeing Billy in tears to the soccer game with a VC head. Billy was so scared he knew no other way out. The game was the anger we all felt so much.

The worst memory for me is the day I sent the 76 men out of your 85 to their deaths. I have to explain and I pray to God you will understand.

At approximately 10:30 am, I watched the tracer rounds from a .50-caliber machine gun firing at our spotter plane. I knew no small group of VC would carry the .50 cal. It wasn't a hit-and-run outfit. I radioed in and by 11:00 the decision was made that you would go for the kill. As I helped you ready for your mission, I recall saying, "I'll see you ugly mugs for lunch." I had no idea you would never eat again.

It wasn't until 3:00 pm that we found out you had walked into an entire regiment of North Vietnamese regulars....It wasn't until the next day that we found out, from a map found on one of the bodies, that it was us they had actually wanted.

All 76 of you died to save the 42 of us.

There are 76 fathers and mothers and God only knows how many wives and children left without you. I live with that thought every day of my life. Many times I have wished I had never seen those tracer rounds fired. To say I was sorry would be an added slap, but sorry I am.

I will never forget my comrades, and I will live with my guilt, sorrow and anger the rest of my life.

My scars can't be seen or touched, but they are deeper than any round that could have been fired.

Dear Bill,

On this Memorial Day 1983, we come to this memorial to
remember and we cry. We come to remember you and all the
young men who died in Vietnam, in a war that was not really
called a war, but a police action.

I and many others cannot understand the reason for it all
but we must try to accept the fact that it did, indeed, happen.
And all that we, the loved ones, can do is to come here and
remember, remember you as a baby, remember your first day
of school, remember the love we shared and remember the
day you died.

Oh, Bill, I miss you so much and the hurt never ends. You
are still with us in our hearts and always will be.

I see your name on a black wall. A name I gave you as
I held you so close after you were born, never dreaming of the
too few years I was to have you. You may be gone, but you are
not by any means forgotten. The love we shared will live on
forever in my heart. You will always be my special love.

And as I look around at the thousands of other names,
I remember that each name here represents, on the average,
20 years that each boy was some Momma's little boy, as you
were mine. I miss you so.

Love, Mom

Although I only met you on a couple of occasions, you were a hero to me. In your uniform, you were the embodiment of an army hero to a seven-year-old child. Little did I know that a few months later you would be killed serving your country.

Without men like you, we couldn't enjoy the lifestyle that we do.

John, you gave your life for us, 21 years old and in your prime. How can we repay you?

We all love you and will always remember your sacrifice.

You are among the giants of our time.

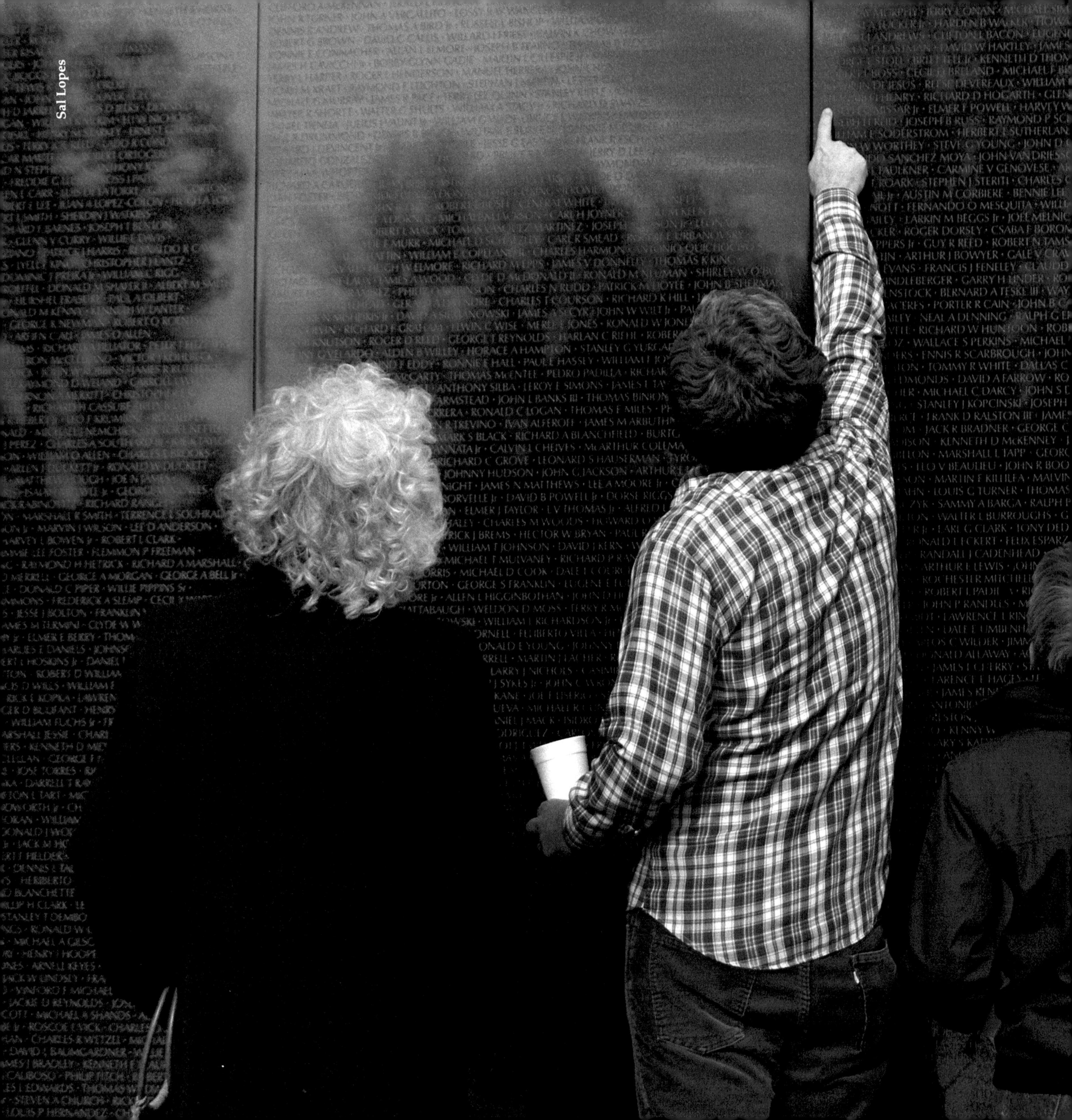

Sal Lopes

How angry I was to find you here, though I knew that you would be. I've wished so hard that I could have saved you. I would give my life if somehow it would bring you all back.

It is only now on my second trip to this monument that I can admit that you, my friends, are gone forever, that I can say your names and speak of your deaths.

I've carried the anguish of your deaths for so long, but I think I can stop looking for you now. I think I can start living without letting you die.

Whenever you start losing a grip,
Remember them guys
Remember those promises,
Even if that's the only thing you stay alive for…
You promised…
You might be the only thing they died for.

I remember your elation on the night we graduated from high school together in 1960.

You and I may not have been the honor students that night but none were more excited about our future. You had chosen military service, I planned service to others through social work.

You gave your life for all of us. Now I'm just a middle-aged woman working daily with people whose youthful dreams have been shattered by life….

99

It's that time of year again for me to say my special hello.
I feel so close to you when I am here at the "Wall." When I see,
feel, and touch your name on this black granite wall, panel
23W, line 57, I feel such pride for having known you for so
many years.

Many times I ask myself why you died and left me behind.
But I will always have the good memories, like the home-
coming dance of '65 when you fell on your behind trying to
impress me with what a good dancer you were.

Remember they called you, me and Jerry Lynn the three
musketeers because when you saw one, you saw all three.
Well, Jerry's name is down on panel 22E, line 46. You two
always did stick together. But you guys left me out this time.

I know you are not lonely in heaven. You have Jerry and
the 58,476 other brothers and sisters whose names are on the
wall with you.

Remember till next year I love and miss you.

Just wanted you to know I love you brother.

Still talk to Cathy and your babies. They're grown and proud of you. You're me, and I'm you. I'll always watch over them for you.

I'll see you soon. Just thought I'd let you know everything is ok.

After you all died, I guess two boyfriends and several friends gone was a bit too much for me and I pretty much screwed up for ten years. Two boyfriends is just too much…too much… too much!

Now I am better. More responsible. I learned that the pain and loss never goes away, it just changes.

Sometimes I think it's more painful now when I'm not "numbed out" on chemicals. And I'm still mad….I have had 20 years now to reflect on this madness and it is always the same.

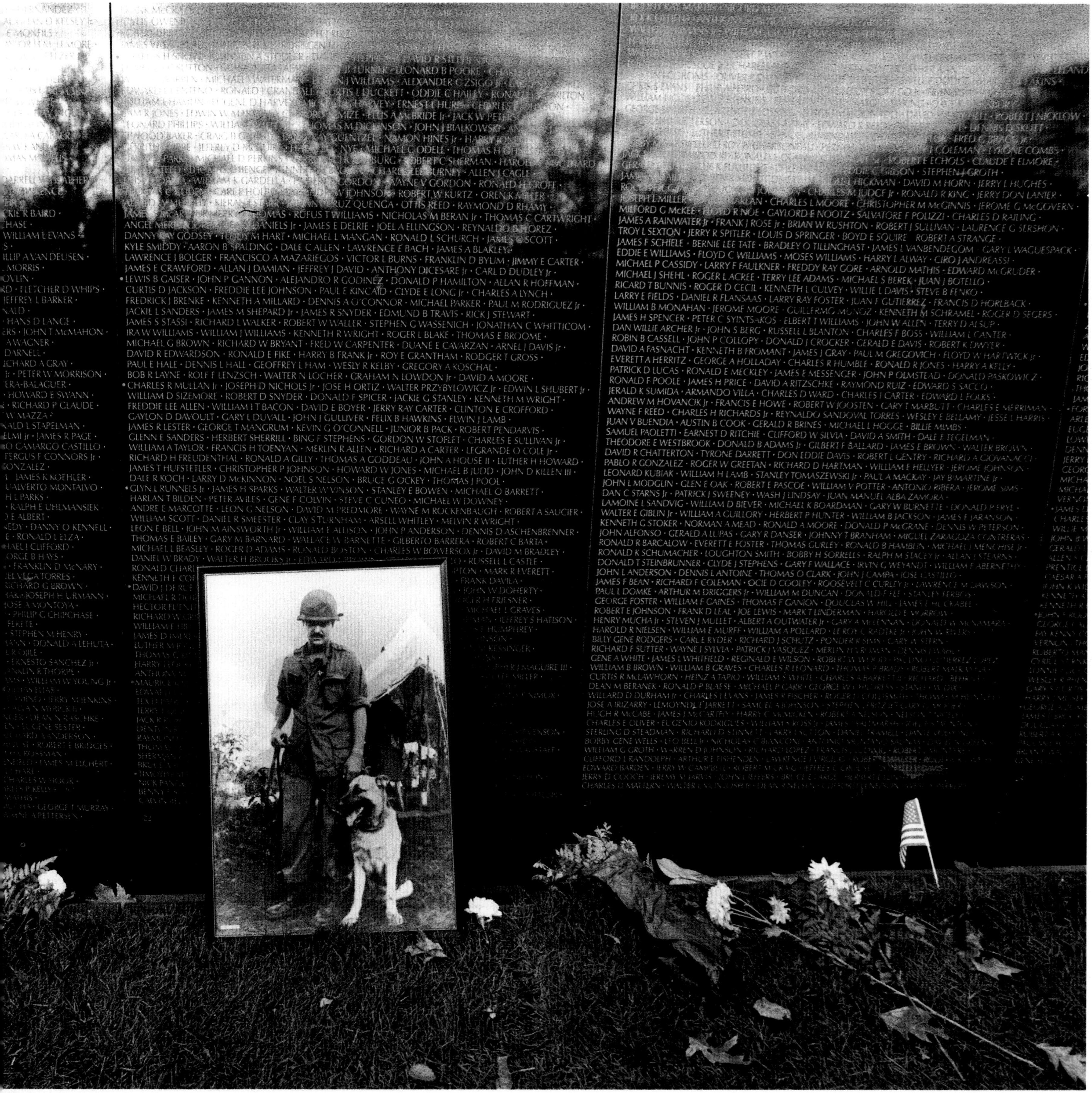

Wendy Watriss

Dearest Eddie Lynn,

I'd give anything to have you shell just one more pecan for me
on Grandma's porch.

All my love,
Your cousin Anne

I have not forgotten you. Nor have I forgotten that you each gave your lives to rescue wounded comrades from a nameless hill in a worthless country. I'm sorry I never wrote your families, but I was wounded myself a few days later and I lost touch with everyone in the hospital.

Now, after 18 years, I have finally begun to write our story. I haven't gotten to March 1, 1968 yet.

I had to come down last night to talk with you before I wrote about that fateful day. I also wanted to spend a little time alone with you on the night before you die again, to be with you when the clock struck midnight and your numbers came up once again. It felt good and I appreciate your talking to me.

Jodi Cobb

I didn't want a monument,
not even one as sober as that
vast black wall of broken lives.
I didn't want a postage stamp.
I didn't want a road beside the Delaware
River with a sign proclaiming:
Vietnam Veterans Memorial Highway.

What I wanted was a simple recognition
of the limits of our power as a nation
to inflict our will on others.
What I wanted was an understanding
that the world is neither black-and-white
nor ours.

What I wanted
was an end to monuments.

Walker,

I miss you dear friend.
Hope things are peaceful for you.

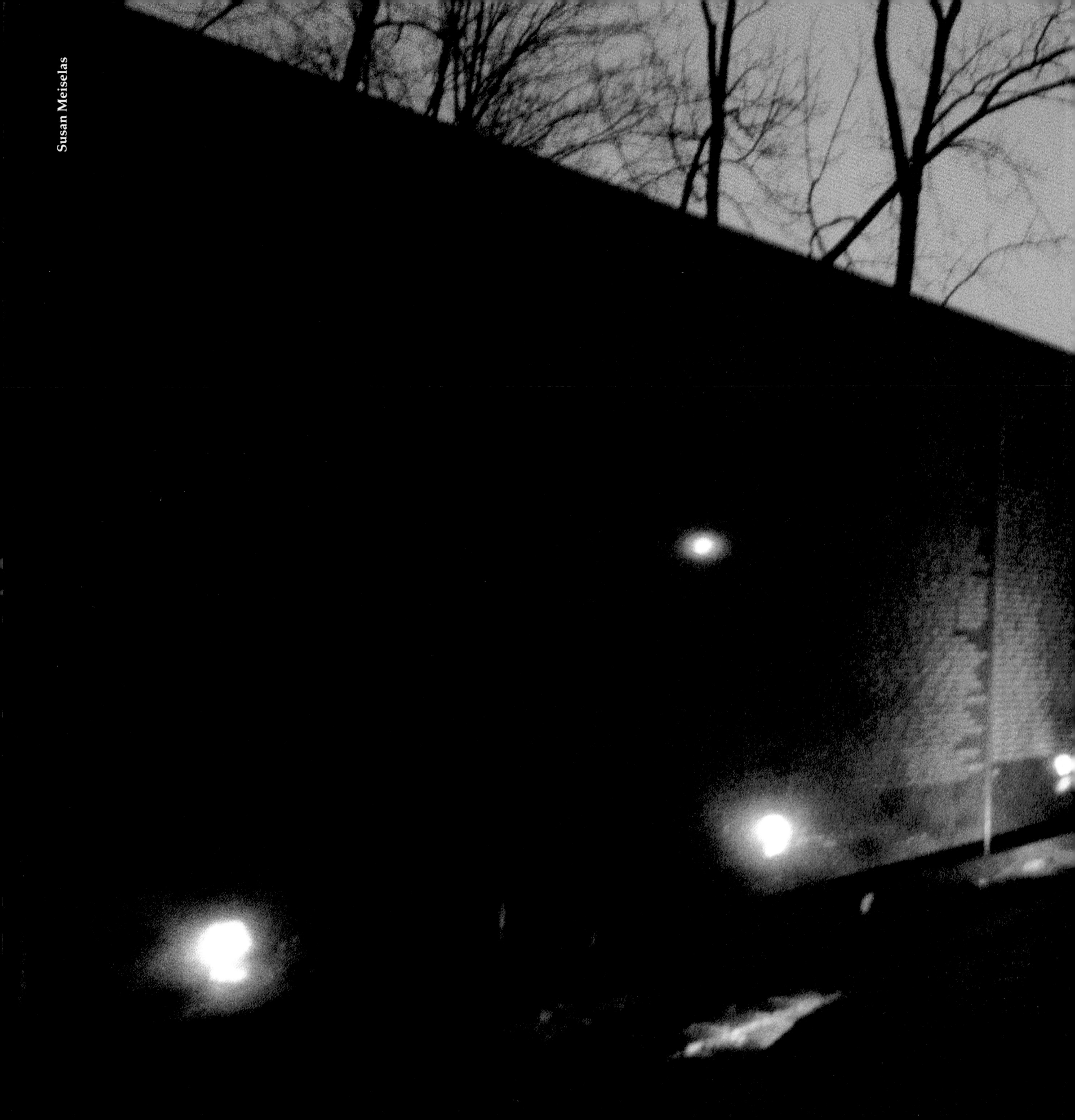

Susan Meiselas

Biographies

Introduction

Michael Norman

Norman is a freelance writer and formerly a correspondent for *The New York Times* where he reported for the Metropolitan News section. He is a frequent contributor to *The New York Times Magazine*. In 1968, Norman served in Vietnam with the U.S. Marine Corps. He is currently writing a book for Crown Publishers on the lives of twelve comrades who served with him during the Vietnam War.

Project Director

Sal Lopes

A freelance photographer based in Boston, Lopes has been photographing the Vietnam Veterans Memorial since its dedication on Veterans Day in 1982. His work on the Wall has been widely published, including photographs in *French Photo, National Geographic*, a Time-Life book series and the book, *To Heal a Nation*.

Photographers

J. Scott Applewhite

Based in Washington, D.C., Applewhite is a staff photographer for the Associated Press. He was awarded first place in news photography by the National Press Photographers Association in 1987 and was a World Press Photo Award winner in 1986. Applewhite was formerly on the staffs of *The Louisville Courier-Journal* and *The Miami Herald*.

Jean-Louis Atlan

Atlan has been a Washington correspondent for Sygma Photos since 1981. Prior to that, he was based in Paris and covered the rise of the Solidarity movement in Poland and the failed rescue mission of the American hostages in Iran. His work has appeared in *Newsweek, Time, Life* and *The New York Times*.

Nathan Benn

A *National Geographic* staff photographer since 1972, Benn's work has also appeared in *Stern, Bunte, Geo* and numerous other magazines. Previously he was a photographer for *The Miami News* and *The Palm Beach Post Times. God of the Country,* Benn's photography book on the Mississippi River, was published in 1985.

Jodi Cobb

Cobb has been a staff photographer for *National Geographic* since 1977. She has produced photographic essays on China, Jerusalem, Jordan and London, and in 1985 she was named the first woman White House Photographer of the Year. She was the subject of the PBS documentary "On Assignment" and was profiled in *American Photographer* in January 1987.

Chuck Fishman

Fishman, a freelance photographer based in New York, works on editorial, corporate and advertising projects worldwide. His photographs have been exhibited in major galleries throughout the world. In 1983, he won two World Press Photo Awards for his photographs of the Wall.

Wally McNamee

McNamee has been a staff photographer with *Newsweek* since 1968 and previously photographed for the U.S. Marine Corps and *The Washington Post*. He is a four-time winner of the White House News Photographers Association Photographer of the Year Award and has won several New York Art Directors' Club citations.

Peter Marlow

Based in London for Magnum Photos, Marlow spends much of his time pursuing personal photographic projects on such topics as the homeless and the unemployed. Currently he is working on two long-term projects on Birmingham and the Thames River. Marlow's photographs have been exhibited widely in Europe.

Susan Meiselas
Meiselas is a photographer for Magnum Photos who has worked extensively in Central America and around the world. Her work has been published in *The New York Times, The London Sunday Times, Epoca* and *Time.* She was awarded the Robert Capa Gold Medal by the Overseas Press Club in 1979 and was named Photojournalist of the Year by the American Society of Magazine Photographers in 1982.

Christopher Morris
A photographer with Black Star photo agency, Morris is regularly on assignment in the Philippines for *Newsweek* and in Central America for *Time.* Based in New York, his work also appears frequently in *Stern, U.S. News & World Report* and *The Christian Science Monitor.*

Seny Norasingh
A frequent contributor to *National Geographic*, Norasingh was previously a staff photographer for *The Raleigh News Observer.* Born and raised in Indochina, he moved to the United States when he was 17. He was twice named North Carolina News Photographer of the Year. Norasingh took the cover photograph of *The Wall* on a 24-hour assignment in the Washington D.C. area for *A Day in the Life of America.*

Eli Reed
Associated with Magnum Photos, Reed's work has appeared regularly in *Time, Life, Newsweek, New York, People* and *Vogue.* A former Nieman Fellow at Harvard, Reed won the 1985 Overseas Press Club Award and the World Understanding Award for his coverage of Central America. He is currently working on a book about the conditions of blacks in North America 20 years after the civil rights movement.

Nick Sebastian
Based in Alexandria, Virginia, Sebastian runs WorldWide Images, a photo news agency. He is a graduate of West Point and holds degrees in law, sociology and engineering. He began his career in photography in 1981.

Charles Tasnadi
Hungarian-born Tasnadi has covered Washington, D.C. for the Associated Press since 1964. He was previously a freelance photographer for Time-Life publications in Venezuela.

Medford Taylor
Taylor is a Black Star photographer whose work frequently appears in *Time, Fortune* and *National Geographic.* He just completed a book project for *National Geographic*, entitled, *Excursion to Enchantment*, on the world's most beautiful places. A naval officer in Vietnam, Taylor began his career in photography when he returned in 1966.

Wendy Watriss
Watriss is a freelance photographer from Houston, Texas, whose photographs have been published in *Life, Geo, The New York Times, Stern* and *Newsweek.* A World Press Photo Award winner, she has received grants from The Rockefeller Foundation and the National Endowment for the Arts. In addition to her work at the Wall, Watriss is currently photographing Vietnam veterans and their Agent Orange-related health problems.

Michael S. Wilson
Wilson's work has been published in *National Geographic*, the *National Parks Magazine* and in publications of the National Parks & History Association. Born in Washington, D.C., Wilson has been a freelance photographer since 1978. He began photographing the Vietnam Veterans Memorial on assignment in 1984.